Collector's Guide to

Country Furniture

Collector's Guide to

Country Furniture

by Don and Carol Raycraft

COLLECTOR BOOKS
A Division of Schroeder Publishing Co., Inc.

The current values in this book should be used only as a guide. They are not intended to set prices, which vary from one section of the country to another. Auction prices as well as dealer prices vary greatly and are affected by condition as well as demand. Neither the Author nor the Publisher assumes responsibility for any losses that might be incurred as a result of consulting this guide.

For Craig, Mike, Scott, and Ben

Acknowledgements

We appreciate the contributions of the following to the development of this book:

Bob and Judy Farling
Gordon and Jean Ann Honegger
Grant Hopkins
Captain Alex Hood
Barb and Dave Bertsche
Jim White
Tom and Becky Heldt
Dennis and Joyce White
Bill Schroeder
Opal and Joe Pickens
Dr. Barry Spitznass

Photography
Carol Raycraft
Miles Bertsche
Bob and Judy Farling
Jean Ann Honegger
Dennis White

Contents

Introduction

It is interesting to spend fifteen minutes with a copy of *Antiques Magazine* from the 1930's or *Hobbies* from the 1950's. The type of items that many of us collect today receive no mention in these publications. Rarely does a search of magazines from the period between 1920 and the mid-1960's turn up an ad for a basket, piece of decorated stoneware, or a bucket bench in its original paint. The country furniture that was offered tended to be refinished and modestly priced.

Serious collectors in the 1920-1960 period tended to search for Pilgrim Century oak and eighteenth century formal furniture. There were few individuals searching for country store advertising items, hooked rugs, and butter molds.

Set of spindle-back kitchen chairs, ca. mid-nineteenth century.

As the supply of seventeenth and eighteenth century antiques dwindled, it was essential that other avenues of collecting be explored. The acceptance of accumulating dry sinks, cupboards, desks, and country side chairs has been slow. Citizens of the eighteenth century who had access to wealth recognized that quality furniture produced by gifted craftsmen should be preserved in elaborate settings. It became fashionable to keep the best of a deceased relative's furnishings away from the village auction block and to sell only the servent's simple pine furniture and extra kitchen utensils.

The household goods of the shop keeper, farmer or shipyard worker in early nineteenth century America were generally acquired through barter with a country carpenter or made at home. Most of the furniture was constructed of pine and it was painted before entering the house.

As the wealth of the family gradually increased, this simple furniture was exchanged for more elaborately designed examples from early factories that produced chairs, beds, desks, and cupboards. After the Civil War the factories that had been created to manufacture uniforms and rifles turned to making household goods on a large scale. Mail order houses were established to bring the products easily and inexpensively to the consumers.

When a couple in Ohio or Michigan received an oak table with claw feet and six leaves by return train from Grand Rapids, they took the handcrafted pine table with a top worn by countless after-dinner scrubbings to the barn where it languished for several generations.

People today are driving hundreds of miles and standing in long lines for an opportunity to purchase the pine table as it is carefully lifted out of that barn.

The photographs in this volume were taken in the homes of collectors and at outdoor antiques shows in New England. We have attempted to show pieces of country furniture that still can be obtained with the expenditure of time and money.

There are a multitude of books that illustrate the best and the brightest from the nation's museums. That is not our intent.

Trends

Collectors of American country antiques from the 1920's through the 1960's had a tendency to separate early furniture from its original finish. If that finish was paint, a mixture of lye and baking soda or a commercial stripper was used. A supply of sandpaper and a belt sander were high on most collectors' Christmas shopping lists. The change to an appreciation for old paint and finishes has been a gradual one, but the numbers of collectors are growing as the quantity of country furniture is rapidly diminishing.

It is interesting to note contemporary furniture advertisements in the numerous home decorating magazines that are displaying lines of "country" furniture with distressed and painted surfaces.

A decade ago it was not uncommon for dealers and collectors of country antiques to drive to the east coast wth an extensive itinary of antiques shops to visit from Pennsylvania to Maine. The change to triple digit gallons of gas and skyrocketing costs of food, lodging, and interest has altered the manner in which many people purchase antiques.

The constraints of time and money have also brought about other changes in the antiques market place. The multitude of outdoor shows involving from fifty to several hundred dealers is interesting to contemplate.

Typically, these shows last a single day with the dealers driving in, setting up, and going home. The dealers' costs are kept to a minimum because they can rent a truck for a day, stock it with furniture, and offer their goods without need for an elaborate booth.

This can be contrasted with the costs incurred when a dealer is faced with an eight hour drive to a three day show that involves food, transportation, booth rent, and lodging. The collector can come to the show and see more dealers in three hours than he could visit in three weeks.

Painted pine dry sink, probably from Pennsylvania, ca. 1850-1870. The dry sink evolved from the bench that was set on the back porch and designed to hold brushes, soap, and buckets on wash day. The front of the bench was eventually enclosed by two doors and zinc was used to line the "well" or trough.

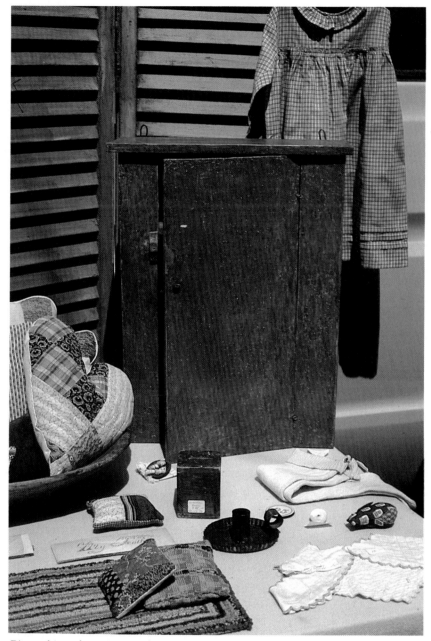

Pine cabinet, late nineteenth century, original blue paint. Unquestionably the most desirable color among collectors of American painted furniture is blue. A cupboard, table, or dry sink in blue paint normally is worth a minimum of 75% more than a similar piece in red or grey.

Painted pine corner cupboard, probably New York state, ca. 1820-1840. A common problem found with cupboards of this type is that they have been stored for lengthy periods of time in a basement or a barn and the exposure to moisture has caused the feet or base to deteriorate. The solution has been to cut off the bracket base and shorten the cupboard. This example has not been cut down and retains its original paint. Corner cupboards with glass panes or "lights" are generally more sought after than "blind" door cupboards.

Pie cupboard, probably from Ohio or Pennsylvania, mid-nineteenth century. There is also a midwestern regional influence on "pie" or kitchen safes. Most of the early examples (1840-1860) were made of pine and contained hand punched tins that allowed air to circulate within the cabinet. This example dates from the 1840-1860 period and is unusual because it has a drawer and storage area below. After the Civil War when factories began to produce furniture and household goods on a large scale, a great many of the safes were made of oak or combinations of pine, poplar, and ash. The tins were machine stamped or screen wire was used to cover circular holes cut in the sides of the safe.

Pie safe, walnut, ca. 1860-1880. This is the standard form that most midwestern safes take. The drawer can be above or below the tins and typically have wooden "mushroom" pulls. These porcelain pulls were a late addition.

Pewter or open cupboard, pine, New England, ca. 1830. Open cupboards are much more difficult to locate than "blind" cupboards with doors but no glass. The desirability of open cupboards has caused restorers on occasion to "lose" the doors of a particularly nice cupboard and fill in the hinge holes with a mixture of glue and saw dust. The filled holes are then carefully painted over to immediately double the price of the cupboard. This is a great early open cupboard with its original paint and the proper amount of wear.

Painted jelly or storage cupboard, pine, probably from Pennsylvania, ca. mid-nineteenth century. Without a doubt the single best assest of this cupboard is the paint. Jelly-type cupboards are not difficult to find and normally are affordable. If this particular cupboard had been refinished and carefully polished with paste wax, its value would be no more than $250.00-$350.00. The century old paint makes it an exceptional piece of country furniture.

Walnut kitchen cupboard, ca. 1875-1890.

Painted pine cupboard, New England, ca. 1830-1850.

Pine jelly cupboard, mustard paint, ca. 1860-1880. In an era when most houses did not contain closets or kitchen cabinets, it was necessary to have a variety of cupboards to store the daily necessities of life.

Pine saw buck table, scrubbed top, New England, ca. mid-nineteenth century. Kitchen tables were in daily use and often were washed and scrubbed down after each meal. A nineteenth century table that was used for eating or food preparation could hardly have much of its original paint left on the two or three board top. The base of the table should still carry at least some remnants of its original color.

Country pine table, turned maple legs, ca. 1850's-1860's.

Pine bucket bench with drawers, late nineteenth century.

Blanket chest, pine, New England, ca. 1820-1840. This early nineteenth century chest could also be called a chest over drawers. The chest has a lift top with two pull out drawers.

Painted blanket chest, pine, bracket feet, New England, ca. 1830.

Painted blanket box, pine, ca. mid-nineteenth century. Six board blanket boxes were commonly used from Indiana to Maine from the early 1800's until the dawn of the twentieth century with little change in construction techniques. Unless it contains cotter pin hinges, wide and irregular dovetails, and a hand wrought lock, the blanket box probably dates from after 1850.

Stack of painted boxes.

Dome top pine boxes from the 1850-1880 period.

Back side of six board blanket box. Exposure to sunlight, dust, and air can gradually turn the white pine back board of a chest almost black over two centuries of use. The interior of a six board chest normally is as unblemished as the day in which it was constructed.

Hitchcock-type chairs, painted, rush seats, New England, ca. 1820-1850. Lambert Hitchcock's chair factory in northwestern Connecticut turned out thousands of hand decorated and stenciled kitchen and "fancy" chairs from the 1820's through the early 1850's. Hitchcock was so successful that numerous other factories adapted his styles. The products were so similar that unless one of Lambert's several trademarks is on the chair it cannot be readily identified as coming from his factory.

Slat or ladder-back chairs, New England, rush seats, mid-nineteenth century. The chairs were sold in sets of 4, 6, 8, or 12. It is almost miraculous for a set of six or eight chairs to have stayed together for over a century without being repainted or extensively repaired. Country side or kitchen chairs were commonly made from a variety of woods that each served a specific purpose in the construction of the chair. Maple and pine were the most commonly used in legs and plank seats.

Mt. Lebanon, New York Shaker rocking chair, ca. late nineteenth century. The Shakers manufactured rocking chairs in eight sizes (0-7) and marketed them thoughout the East in the late nineteenth and early twentieth century. The chairs were made from maple and were available in several colors. The Shakers began to issue catalogs that illustrated the variety of types and sizes of chairs that could be mail ordered in the 1870's.

Variety of Shaker rocking chairs, Mt. Lebanon, New York, late nineteenth century.

Pine hanging cupboard, painted grey, ca. late nineteenth century. It is interesting to note the cleats or battens across the back of the cupboard's door.

Pine dry sink, ca. late nineteenth century. If two doors were added to the bottom section, this would be a conventional dry sink with a deep trough.

Miniature pine blanket chest, lift top, original painted finish, ca. 1820-1830, "boot jack" ends on the side boards. In New England this form is sometimes described as a "chest over drawer."

Nineteenth century pine cupboards. The pine cupboard in the center is a "blind front" and also a "step-back." A "step-back" cupboard has a bottom section that is 6" to 12" deeper than the upper portion of the cupboard. This provided an additional storage area or a shelf for food preparation.

Pine open cupboard, Queen Anne tea table, bannister-back chair, all late eighteenth-
early nineteenth century.

Pine "step-back" cupboard, painted, ca. 1840-1860.

Ladder-back children's chairs, nineteenth century.

Country Furniture

We have been collecting country antiques for a long time. In the early 1960's we searched for books that could assist us in our quest for the cupboards, dry sinks, and wash benches that only recently have been "discovered" by the home decorating magazines. There was not a wealth of material available to read twenty years ago but there were classic books by Arthur Hayward on lighting and Mary Earle Gould on woodenware that kept us hungry. Both authors combined information about their collections with stories of the "hunt" and the interesting people they encountered along the way.

It is worthwhile to note that Hayward's book, written in the 1920's, warns collectors of that period to be wary of fakes. It is equally interesting to speculate how many of those sixty year old fakes have become the focal points of major collections today.

Perhaps the best part of collecting for many people is the "hunt." I can remember as a child standing in a checkout line at a local Kroger store with a pack of 1953 Topps baseball cards and a nickel, waiting to get outside to rip open the wrapper and find a Mickey Mantle. Typically, I found doubles of Willie Miranda, Rip Repulski, and Craig Bazzani rather than a Mantle, but that moment of anticipation spent fumbling through the cards and the periodic rush of success that followed has stayed with me for thirty years. Our children now buy their baseball cards by the set rather than by rolling the dice each time they purchase a single pack. They get no duplicate cards but they also miss the joy of standing in the checkout line and listening to their hearts beat.

We have a close friend who is a gifted surgeon and deals with life and death on a daily basis. The night before an antiques show he finds the anticipation of what he might find the next day so great that the anxiety it generates keeps him from sleeping. Most of the time he finds nothing that interests him but the anxiety and anticipation linger on and keep bringing him back.

Shaker chest of drawers from Enfield, Connecticut and a stack of painted firkins or sugar buckets from the late nineteenth century.

Shaker tilter chair, ladder-back, flame finials, original finish, replaced taped seat, Mt. Lebanon, New York.

Shaker dry sink, Enfield, Connecticut, nineteenth century.

Shaker milk keeler. In an era before there was a convenience store on most street corners, milk was a treasured commodity in most nineteenth century homes. A keeler was a staved tub that was filled with freshly "pulled" milk that was given an opportunity to cool. The keeler is made of pine with "lappers" or fingers held by copper nails. Two of the staves are extended to form a set of piggin handles. A broom stick could be inserted between the handles and the keeler could be transported. The lathe-turned wooden bowls were factory made in the 1870-1900 period.

Shaker weaver's chair, ladder-back with turned arms, painted a worn brown, New England, mid-nineteenth century.

Shaker blanket box, pine, mid-nineteenth century, New England. The Shakers used peg rails in their buildings to hang chairs when they were not in use. The rails were nailed six feet from the floor and made of pine. The pegs were lathe turned of pine or maple and often were threaded. It is difficult to find peg rails in quantity. Most were ripped from the walls when the Shaker buildings were torn down or recycled into laundromats. The rails that have survived are found in odd lengths and usually without several of their original pegs.

Pine chest of drawers, Shaker, New England, mid-nineteenth century. Case pieces of Shaker furniture in early paint are uncommonly found. This pine, three drawer chest dates from about 1860 and carries its original coat of blue paint. It is usually difficult to isolate in which specific Shaker community a piece of furniture was made because as the communities closed, the brothers and sisters took their furnishings and moved to a surviving colony.

Painted dry sink and splint cheese basket, nineteenth century. If one of the goals of your life is to separate the curds from the whey, it is essential that you find a cheese basket. When the typical cheese or curd basket reached the $350.00 plateau, a large number of contemporary counterfeits made their way to the market place. The hexagon or "cheese" weave was also used in herb drying baskets by the Shakers and other nineteenth century basket makers. The pine dry sink was purchased in Ohio but probably originally came from Pennsylvania. The extended "well" or trough makes it an unusual example.

Pine dry sink and painted chopping bowl, mid-nineteenth century. The rectangular handcrafted bowl with red paint was found in Ohio and dates from about 1850. The pine dry sink is a form that is found more often in New York state than in the Midwest. The dry sink that later evolved from this form had the frame enclosed and two doors added onto the front.

Country dry sink, great blue paint, ca. 1870's, found in Ohio.

Pine open cupboard, painted red, ca. mid-nineteenth century. It is essential that you check an open front cupboard carefully for traces of hinges that originally held a set of doors. When the doors are broken or lost it is relatively simple to remove the hinges, fill in the nail or screw holes, and create an open cupboard in "original" condition.

Step-back pine cupboard, "blind front," replaced "shoe" feet, mid-nineteenth century.

Step-back cupboard, painted, found in southern Indiana, ca. 1840-1860.

Linen press, Pennsylvania, ca. 1830-1850, original grey paint. A "press" is a nineteenth century term for a storage cupboard.

Pine cupboard, Ohio, mid-nineteenth century. A glazed front country cupboard contains doors with individual panes of glass. This "blind" front cupboard has no "lights" or panes of glass but it does have its original paint. It was necessary to gradually strip away the latest, later, and late paint to get down to the original washed out orange. The cupboard was made in two pieces so it could be easily moved. Many early cupboards were constructed in two sections so they could be loaded into a Conestoga wagon and carted on down the road.

Cant-back cupboard, Connecticut, grained decoration, early nineteenth century.

Refinished pine storage cupboard or "jam" cupboard, probably midwestern, ca. second half of the nineteenth century.

Tavern table, pine top and tiger maple base, ca. late eighteenth-early nineteenth century. The four gallon jug is unusual because it has an elaborate scene brush-painted on its surface. It was produced after 1850 at the New York Stoneware Company, Ft. Edward, New York.

New England saw buck table, pine, scrubbed top, ca. 1850.

Ladder-back country side chair, ca. 1860's.

Slat or ladder-back rocking chairs, Shaker, Mt. Lebanon, New York, late nineteenth century.

Painted rocking chair from Zoar, Ohio, late nineteenth century. Rocking chairs are alledged to have first been used in the American colonies in the mid-eighteenth century. The earliest rocking chairs were fashioned from straight chairs. This nursing or sewing rocker is a ladder or slat-back with red paint. It has a replaced seat of wool tapes. The original seat was probably made of oak or ash splint. The primary wood in the chair is maple.

Arrow-back rocking chair, stenciled decoration, ca. mid-nineteenth century.

Rare #1 child's Shaker arm chair, Mt. Lebanon, New York, ca. 1870-1900.

Ladder-back side chair, replaced splint seat, early red paint. Chairs were normally made in sets of four to twelve. Relatively few complete sets have survived but it is not uncommon to find a pair of country side chairs for sale in an antiques shop. This chair was not made in an early factory but created by a long forgotten wood turner who was probably paid in bacon or cheese for his efforts.

Pine chair table, New England, ca. 1840.

Pine cradle, painted "Indian" red, ca. 1835-1850, New England.

Mammy's bench, stenciled crest rail, factory made, original gate to hold a child, ca. 1850-1860.

Pine cradle, originally from Maine, ca. 1870's. We found the pine cradle at Brimfield, Massachusetts in the summer of 1981. A dealer from Maine said that he had purchased it out of the attic of a farm house near Portland the week before. It is not an exceptionally early piece nor is the form especially unusual. The premier attribute it carries is the great orange paint. The series of flea markets at Brimfield in the spring, summer, and fall is worth the trip if only to see what America's basement and unclaimed freight store really look like. Brimfield is the K Mart on Saturday night with blue light specials that last nine days.

Low post rope bed, pine and maple, original red paint, found in Pennsylvania, ca. 1860's.

Painted country bed, found in Maine, ca. 1830-1850.

Bentwood cradle, late nineteenth century.

Ohio bucket bench, pine, late nineteenth century. Shaker tilter chair, Mt. Lebanon, New York. "Jacob's coat" quilt, Berks County, Pennsylvania, ca. 1890.

New York State bucket bench, red painted pine, ca. mid-nineteenth century.

Collection of painted firkins and pantry boxes stacked on two bucket benches.

The combinations of colors can literally light up a room. In building stacks of pantry boxes and firkins the smallest sizes are usually the most difficult to find.

Stack of miniature boxes in early paint.

Pine storage boxes from New England, nineteenth century.

Pine apothecary chest, New England, nineteenth century.

Rocking butter churn found in Pennsylvania.

Shaker carrier with fingers or "lappers," late nineteenth century.

Pine apothecary chest from a New England country store, mid-nineteenth century.

Painted pine desk, stenciled decoration, probably from Pennsylvania, mid-nineteenth century.

Sea chest, pine, found in New Hampshire, late nineteenth century.

Dome top pine trunk, sponge decorated, ca. 1820-1840.

Smalls

If you are going to collect American country furniture to decorate a home in Hawaii, an apartment in Arkansas, or a condo in Colorado, it is equally as important to find decorated stoneware, baskets, textiles, and woodenware to complete the setting.

These accessories or "smalls" usually are more difficult to find than a painted dry sink or saw buck table. They were used on a daily basis and were subjected to significant abuse. Relatively few stoneware jugs, splint baskets, or quilts have survived unscathed.

If the bottom of a basket was gone or the strap handle of a jug was broken off, little attempt at repair was made. These items were utilitarian and readily replaceable from a local basket weaver or potter. Unfortunately today the tinker, the candlestick maker, and most of the bakers have long ago caught the last train for the coast.

Variety of early basket forms, nineteenth century.

Cast iron windmill weight and sheet metal jockey, ca. 1880-1900. In the late 1960's we were driving home from Denver and stopped at an isolated exit somewhere in Nebraska for some gasoline and a Milky Way. As we left the gas station, we noticed a small weathered sign and an arrow that read "Antiques- one mile." We followed a gravel road and came upon a farm house and an elderly woman mowing her lawn. We noticed that the front yard was filled with cast iron horses, chickens, and cows similar in size to the example illustrated here. She told us that the iron figures were windmill weights that were found in Nebraska and the Dakotas at the turn of the century. We felt obligated to buy something from her shop but found only depression glass, dishes, and a button hook collection. We did the lady a favor and bought two of the weights for $20.00 each out of her front yard. A year later we saw some similar examples advertised for $300.00-$350.00 each in the *Maine Antiques Digest*. We tried to do her several more favors but we could not find the business card that would relocate her front yard. We did find the Milky Way wrappers under the front seat.

Stack of seed boxes, late nineteenth century. There is a tendency for collectors to have been perpetual keepers of memorabilia since the eighth grade picnic. You reach a point where one seed box (pantry box, basket) leads to a dozen and stacks are born.

Stack of Shaker seed boxes, nineteenth century. The Shakers were in the seed business for almost a century. They were the first to offer individual packets or "papers" filled with seeds. Other growers sold only in bulk.

Late nineteenth century shopkeepers received most products in boxes ready for display on their counters.

Melon basket, oak splint, ca. late nineteenth century. Most country baskets were not made for a specific purpose. They were designed for gathering (eggs, apples, potatoes), storage, or for setting in a corner. The melon shaped basket form was ideal for use in any situation where light loads needed to be transported.

Splint apple drying basket, oak and pine frame. Baskets designed for specific pur-
poses like separating cheese curds from whey or drying apples should contain
some evidence of the use to which they were put. The splint in the basket is heavi-
ly stained from contact with the apple slices. The pig could be an excellent source
of bacon on a cold winter's morning, but it isn't.

Laundry sign, pine, ca. 1915. This laundry sign was originally hinged on the top, backed with another sign, and placed on the sidewalk in front of the store for passersby to stumble over.

Bank sign, originally from Ohio but purchased in Vermont, late nineteenth century.

Nineteenth century game board, pine, New England.

Country baskets have escalated dramatically in price over the past decade. Swing handle baskets that were $45.00-$55.00 in the mid-1970's are now approaching $300.00.

Pine garden carrier filled with treenware.

Stack of pantry boxes in a variety of colors, maple and pine, late nineteenth century.

Nineteenth century stoneware with cobalt blue decoration.

A young boy and his well-cared-for pet.

Folk Art

Books and doctoral dissertations have been written about precisely what the field of "folk art" encompasses. The two Uncle Sam plant stands could almost serve as a definition. They were carved from a single block of wood by Indiana farmer, John Horney, in the early twentieth century. Horney died in 1942.

John Horney, like most folk artists, was self-taught and produced his carvings for his own amusement and as gifts for his children and friends.

Few potters, basketmakers, wood carvers, or painters had any degree of popularity or fame during their life times. The majority created their art in almost total obscurity and remain anonymous today.

Hand-carved Uncle Sam.

Close-up of Uncle Sam carved by John Horney.

Another Uncle Sam plant stand hand-carved by John Horney.

Country Christmas

Christmas is a special time for collectors of country antiques. The traditions of the season blend naturally with the worn surfaces of pine furniture and the reflected glow of countless late night fires from copper kettles and "glazed" cupboards.

At our house the tree goes up in early December and the wreaths come down in March. They may be found on doors of all sizes, in baskets, and hanging from windows.

The tulips are usually breaking through cracks in the ground before the wreath is taken down each year.

We had to go to at least six bird house shops before we could find a wreath that fit.

The horse dates from the late nineteenth century. It can be taken off the rockers and rolled on its cast iron wheels.

A simple wreath made from pine branches with a red bow and a fresh snow fall symbolize the season.

The splint field basket was used in the nineteenth century for gathering garden vegetables. In the late twentieth century it is used for displaying a Christmas wreath.

Terms

If you are going to collect American country furniture it is essential that you have an emergency vocabulary of at least twenty terms to fall back upon when you want to ask a dealer a question or start a conversation with a fellow collector.

As found-The condition the piece appeared in immediately after being hauled out of an attic or barn, not restored.

Back Boards-Literally the boards on the back or reverse side of a case piece of furniture.

Bread board end-A strip of wood nailed or mortised to the end of a table top to keep it from warping.

Case piece-A desk, cupboard, piesafe, chest of drawers.

Crest rail-The top slat on a ladder-back chair, often stenciled.

Dovetail-A type of joint used by cabinet makers to hold two pieces of wood together at a corner.

Finial-The decorative turning at the top of the back post of a chair.

Grain painted-A decorative technique used to simulate the wood grain of mahogany, rosewood, etc., often done over pine.

Marriage-The combination of two or more pieces of furniture to form a single desk, cupboard, bed. Generally done to deceive a prospective buyer into thinking the piece is original.

Original-Untouched, not refinished or reworked in any way.

Patina-The natural finish on a piece of furniture of woodenware that is created by a combination of wear and exposure to sunlight and dust over a long period of time.

Picker-An individual who spends a great deal of time on the road buying and selling antiques to dealers.

Pieced out-A carpentry technique used to add height to a chair or table. A chair or table that has had restoration to its legs to restore a portion that might of been cut down or damaged is said to have been "pieced out."

Provenance-A history of the ownership of the antique. Generally, an oral history rather than a documented one.

Score marks-marks that go completely around a chair leg or back post to show where slats or rungs should be placed.

Scribe mark-A straight line on a drawer side to mark the depth of a dovetail.

Scrub top-A table top that has lost its paint from repeated after-meal "scrubbings" over a long period of time.

Skinned-Refinished to the point where all patina and signs of wear are erased forever. Generally a derogatory term for a piece that has been overly refinished.

Treenware-Woodware, usually a kitchen implement made of wood.

Turned-Often a table leg or chair post or leg that has been shaped on a lathe.

Pine table with scrubbed top and "bread board" ends, early nineteenth century. Bow-back Windsor side chair, variety of woods, ca. 1800-1830.

Pine blanket box, grained finish, ca. 1840-1860. The oak graining on this six-board pine blanket box from the mid-nineteenth century was probably added in the 1870-1890 period. As factory produced oak became popular, a large number of earlier pine country pieces were grain painted to resemble the more fashionable oak.

"Scrub top" saw buck table, pine, painted base, early nineteenth century. It would be an impossibility for a nineteenth century work or dining table to survive with its original paint intact. The process of washing down the table top after each meal gradually takes its toll.

Set of "skinned" chairs. The cast iron horse is a windmill weight and the copper cow is from a late nineteenth century weathervane.

Parts

There are some basic indicators of age in most pieces of country furniture that even neophyte collectors can ascertain before they write the check and add a chair or cupboard to their permanent collection. Even a cursory inspection of the "parts" of a chest or dry sink can be beneficial before you tie it to the top of the car.

Tool Marks
Wood purchased from lumber yards today is pre-cut to dimension and planed to a satin smooth finish. Prior to the 1870's householders or carpenters bought their lumber at a mill and used a jack plane to smooth the rough cut boards. The jack plane and the smaller finishing planes left slight ridges and valleys on the boards that were caused by unevenly applied pressure during the hand planing process.

In attempting to date a cupboard, one of the initial places to check should be on the back boards. If the piece dates from before the mid-point of the nineteenth century the boards on the back of the cupboard should show evidence of being hand planed. The underside of early table tops should also have a similar appearance.

Even if the cupboard has been stripped of its early finish, sanded, varnished, and waxed, the boards on the back probably have not been touched and will show evidence of hand planing if they were milled before the 1870's.

Dovetails
A dovetail is a common technique used by craftsmen to join corners of drawers and blanket chests. Dovetails were also used on case pieces (desks, cupboards) to join the top with a side. The earliest pieces of American country furniture contained dovetails that were much larger in size and fewer in number than later factory produced dovetails.

When a dovetail was handmade it was necessary for the cabinet maker to mark the depth of his cut. Typically, he used a nail or a sharp tool called a scribe to make a thin line on the side of the drawer. Scribe marks are *only* found on drawers with hand done dovetails. A dovetail machine did not need a line to mark the depth of its cut.

In the late 1880's furniture factories begain to use machines that stamped out precut drawer sides for easy assembly. If a piece of furniture has dovetailed drawers but no scribe marks, it is a probability that it was made *after* 1890.

The earliest furniture factories (ca. 1830's) combined hand work with machines to produce sets of chairs. After the Civil War when the mail order houses began to mass produce furniture, the work of the individual craftsmen was largely gone.

Hand done dovetails on painted pine box. The scribe marks are barely visible under the blue paint of the pine box. Dovetails created by nineteenth century cabinet makers were irregular in size and also in the distance between each one.

etailed drawer with scribe
k that indicated how deep
cabinet maker's cut should

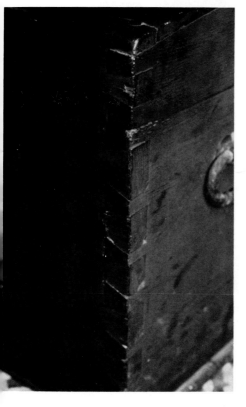

Dovetailed corner on early
nineteenth century sea captain's chest.

Factory or machine-made dovetail on late nineteenth century seed box. Note how each dovetail is the same size and an equal distance apart.

Score Marks

A score mark is a line that goes completely around a lathe- turned chair leg or post to indicate to the cabinet maker precisely where the mortise cuts were to be made so chair slats or rungs could be inserted.

The score marks were made while the piece was being turned out on the lathe. On factory made chairs there was no need for score marks. A chair with score marks can be dated in a similar fashion as a cupboard with dovetailed drawers and scribe marks. Few chairs with score marks were produced after the 1880-1890 period.

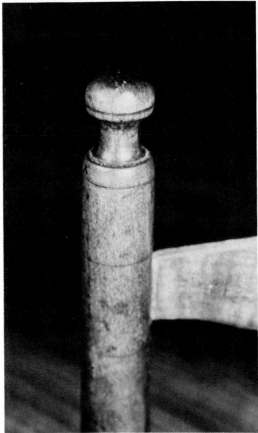

Score marks on a post served as a guide for the chair maker when he cut the mortise hole.

Pins

Country cabinet makers used a variety of techniques to hold their creations together. It is not uncommon to find a six board blanket box or chest with the boards "butted" up against each other and nailed. The obvious problem with "butt" construction is that over time the boards shrink, crack, and eventually split around the nails.

The wooden pins were made of hard wood and used to hold mortise and tenon joints together. They were intentionally cut in an irregular way so they would bite into the wood of the joint and hold it tightly together. As the wood shrinks, the wooden pins or pegs are gradually squeezed or forced above the surface of the joint and usually are readily visible.

A "pin top" on a table or a protruding pin on a chair post often indicate the piece was made prior to the 1850's. When the furniture factories began to mass produce their wares after the Civil War it was no longer necessary to use wooden pins. The chair factories used glue rather than pins to hold the slats into the posts.

Wooden pin inserted in back of chair post to hold the tenon in the mortise. The shrinkage of the wood over time has raised the wooden pin above the surface of the post.

Screws

Nineteenth century cabinet makers often used screws to secure hinges or even to hold a top to the apron of a table.

Hand forged screws are also an obvious aid to dating a piece of country furniture. The threads are always uneven and the slot for the screw driver is off center, shallow, and narrow. The ends of the screws were cut off and blunt rather than pointed. Early screws also tend to be relatively short and seldom more than ½″ in length. Screws made after 1870 resemble those of today with pointed or gimlet ends.

Glass

Glass used in nineteenth century "glazed" cupboards made before 1850 contained wavy lines, ripples, and small bubbles. It is highly unlikely that a cupboard with sixteen "lights" could have survived with all of its original glass intact.

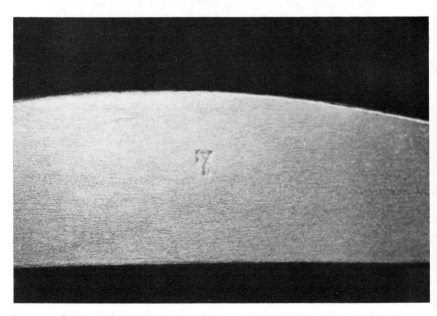

Impressed "7" in the back of a top slat on a Shaker rocking chair. The Shakers were in the chair business for more than a century. They produced chairs of maple in eight sizes (0-7) for sale to the "world." The "production" rocking chairs were available in several colors by mail order or in department stores east of the Mississippi River. The community at Mt. Lebanon, New York was the center of the Shaker chair-making industry.

Arrow-back chair, pine and maple, ca. 1850. This chair was covered with a coat of red primer and then painted a dark brown and stenciled. It is interesting to note the wear on the seat and the remainder of the chair that came in direct contact with a constant stream of buttocks and backs. If the pine plank seat was still covered with its "original" paint that showed no sign of wear, the potential buyer should have some serious skepticism about its authenticity.

Top of pine bench showing an open mortise and tenon joint.

"Flame" finial on Shaker rocking chair.

Slat-back or ladder-back country rocking chair from Ohio, mid-nineteenth century.

Crudely executed finial on back post of Ohio rocking chair.

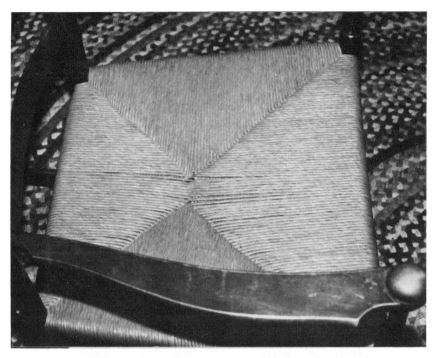

Rush seat of Shaker rocking chair. Most nineteenth century straight chairs or
rocking chairs had seats made of rush, oak or ash splint, or a 2″ thick pine plank.

Splint seat of Shaker chair, woven in "twill" pattern.

Late nineteenth century log chair with seat of thickly cut oak splints.

Hand wrought iron lock on miniature pine chest.

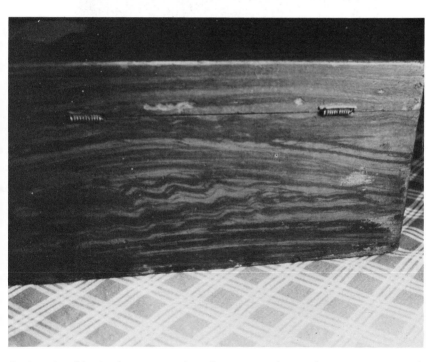

Grain painted back of miniature chest done to simulate mahogany or rosewood.

Price List

There are wide variations of price and demand for country furniture across the nation. These estimation represent current "ball park" evaluations. They should serve only as a guide to value.

Page 11
Pine dry sink - $750.00-900.00

Page 12
Pine cabinet - $250.00-275.00

Page 13
Pine corner cupboard - $1600.00-2000.00

Page 14
Pie cupboard - $600.00-800.00

Page 15
Pie safe - $225.00-350.00

Page 16
Pine open cupboard - $2800.00-3500.00

Page 17
Painted jelly cupboard - $600.00-800.00
Walnut kitchen cupboard - $300.00-400.00

Page 18
Painted pine cupboard - $700.00-875.00

Page 19
Pine jelly cupboard - $500.00-700.00
Pine saw buck table - $800.00-1200.00

Page 20
Pine table - $500.00-750.00
Pine bucket bench - $300.00-475.00

Page 21
Blanket chest - $1400.00-2000.00
Painted chest w/bracket feet - $1200.00-1800.00

Page 22
Painted blanket box - $225.00-350.00
Stack of painted boxes - $225.00-375.00

Page 23
Dome top boxes - $200.00-350.00
Six board blanket box -
$300.00-425.00

Page 24
Four painted chairs -
$750.00-1000.00
Four ladder-back chairs -
$700.00-1000.00

Page 25
Shaker rocking chair -
$600.00-750.00
Variety of Shaker chairs -
$400.00-850.00

Page 26
Pine hanging cupboard -
$225.00-325.00
Pine dry sink - $550.00-800.00

Page 27
Miniature chest - $650.00-950.00
Pine cupboards - $1500.00-3500.00

Page 28
Pine open cupboard -
$2800.00-3500.00

Page 29
"Step-back" cupboard -
$800.00-1300.00

Page 30
Ladder-back children's chairs -
$100.00-250.00 each

Page 32
Shaker chest - $8000.00-10,000.00
Tilter chair - $900.00-$1100.00

Page 33
Shaker dry sink - $2500.00-3000.00
Shaker milk keeler - $550.00-650.00

Page 34
Weaver's chair - $600.00-750.00

Page 35
Shaker blanket box -
$1000.00-1200.00

Page 36
Blue 3 drawer chest -
$1100.00-1300.00

Page 37
Dry sink - $700.00-950.00
N.Y. State dry sink - $575.00-750.00

Page 38
Blue dry sink - $650.00-750.00

Page 39
Pine open cupboard -
$1300.00-1600.00

Page 40
Step-back pine cupboard -
$1200.00-1400.00

Page 41
Indiana step-back cupboard -
$1450.00-1750.00

Page 42
PA linen press - $2500.00-3000.00
Child's high chair - $375.00-500.00

Page 43
"Blind" front cupboard -
$1200.00-1400.00

Page 44
  Cant-back cupboard -
  $4500.00-5500.00

Page 45
  Refinished pine storage cupboard -
  $400.00-600.00

Page 46
  Tavern table - $1500.00-2000.00
  Stoneware jug - $850.00-950.00

Page 47
  Small saw buck table -
  $500.00-600.00

Page 48
  Slat-back chair - $115.00-130.00
  Slat-back rocking chairs -
  $650.00-1200.00

Page 49
  Zoar rocking chair - $200.00-225.00

Page 50
  Arrow-backing chair - $250.00-300.0

Page 51
  #1 Child's Shaker chair -
  $800.00-1100.00

Page 52
  Ladder-back side chair -
  $100.00-125.00

Page 53
  Pine chair table - $1400.00-1700.00

Page 54
  "Indian" red cradle - $400.00-550.00

Page 55
  Mammy's bench - $600.00-900.00
  Orange cradle - $400.00-500.00

Page 56
  Low post bed - $700.00-900.00
  Painted bed - $700.00-1000.00

Page 57
  Bentwood cradle - $200.00-275.00

Page 58
  "Jacob's coat" quilt -
  $3000.00-3500.00
  Ohio bucket bench - $500.00-700.0

Page 59
  Bucket bench - $700.00-900.00
  Bucket benches - $750.00-950.00

Page 60
  Firkins - $110.00-200.00

Page 61
  Miniature boxes - $110.00-145.00

Page 62
  Storage boxes - $200.00-400.00

Page 63
  Apothecary chest -
  $2000.00-2500.00

Page 64
  Rocking butter churn -
  $300.00-450.00

Page 65
  Shaker carrier - $1750.00-2450.0
  Apothecary chest -
  $2000.00-2500.00

Page 66
PA desk - $1000.00-1500.00

Page 67
Sea chest - $500.00-600.00
Dome top pine trunk -
$350.00-500.00

Page 68
Variety of early basket forms -
$200.00-450.00

Page 69
Windmill weight - $500.00-650.00

Page 70
Stack of seed boxes - $200.00-350.00

Page 71
Stack of Shaker seed boxes -
$300.00-450.00

Page 72
Boxes - $45.00-75.00

Page 73
Melon basket - $125.00-150.00

Page 74
Apple drying basket -
$300.00-400.00

Page 75
Laundry sign - $250.00-325.00

Page 76
Bank sign - $600.00-750.00

Page 77
Game board - $325.00-350.00

Page 78
Assorted baskets - $300.00-325.00
Garden box - $125.00-150.00

Page 79
Stack of Pantry boxes -
$100.00-225.00 each

Page 80
Stoneware - $100.00-200.00

Sources

There are articles in many magazines each month that point out great books, inns, bed and breakfast stops, restaurants, and suggested field trips. The problem develops when everyone who reads the articles converges on what ever is reviewed on the same weekend.

We have listed below some places, periodicals, and books with which you might want to spend some time. Several of the books, newspapers, and magazines may already have a prominent spot in your antiques library.

The list of suggested reading includes a book on early lighting, Shaker and country furniture, decorated stoneware, woodenware, baskets, a price guide to country antiques, and a source book to interior design.

Places

We have selected the museums and restorations below after a great deal of consideration. Each is readily accessible and provides the type of atmosphere conducive to children. It is possible in each to walk from building to building at your leisure. There are no tour guides and time limits to stand in the way of your enjoyment. We have never faced significant crowds at any of the five.

Shelburne Museum
Rt. 7
Shelburne, VT   05482

Shelburne is unique because of the relaxed atmosphere it provides visitors and the incredible collection of collections it houses. On the way up to Shelburne you will probably pass through Rutland, Vermont and have the opportunity to savor America's premier donut at the Jones Bakery (one block east of Rt. 7).

The Farmer's Museum
Cooperstown, NY   13326

Cooperstown and Shelburne are towns that you do not normally pass on the way to somewhere else. You truly have to want to go to both. The Farmer's Museum houses the Cardiff Giant and a variety of other nineteenth century farm related displays. Cooperstown is also the home of major league baseball's Hall of Fame and is one of the nation's truly great small towns that has not yet sold out to the temptations of commercialism.

Shaker Museum
Shaker Museum Road
Old Chatham, NY   12136

This museum contains one of the wold's largest collection of Shaker case pieces, baskets, tools, bottles, and kitchen utensils. It is also only a few miles from the Hancock Shaker restoration just west of Pittsfield, MA.

Shaker Village - Pleasant Hill
Rt. 4
Harrodsburg, KY   40330

It is a rare opportunity to walk the grounds of a former Shaker village and experience the stone fences, buildings, and collection of furnishings. The village is located east of Harrodsburg and provides the visitor with accomodations for lodging and dining in a restored Shaker building.

Pennsylvania Farm Museum of Landis Valley
2451 Kiddel Hill Road
Lancaster, PA   17601

This museum is surrounded by several of our favorite places. The Black Angus Weekend Antiques Mart and the Green Dragon Farmer's Market are located north of Landus Valley about fifteen minutes away. The Green Dragon is open only on Fridays and is a rewarding experience.

Periodicals

Maine Antiques Digest, Waldoboro, Maine   (published 11 times each year)

Ohio Antiques Review, Worthington, Ohio   (published 11 times each year)

Antiques and Arts Weekly, Newtown, Connecticut   (52 issues a year)

Schroeder's Insider, Paducah, Kentucky   (published 12 times each year)

Books

Emmerling, Mary, *American Country - A Style and Source Book,* Clarkson N. Potter Inc.

Gould, Mary Earle, *Early American Wooden Ware,* Tuttle.

Kassay, John, *The Book of Shaker Furniture,* U. of Massachusetts Press.

Pain, Howard, *The Heritage of Country Furniture,* Van Nostrand Reinhold.

Raycraft, Don and Carol, *Wallace-Homestead Price Guide to American Country Antiques,* Wallace-Homestead.

The Rush Light Club, *Early Lighting: A Pictorial Guide.*

Teleki, Gloria, *Baskets of Rural America,* E.P. Dutton.

Webster, Donald Blake, *Decorated Stoneware Pottery of North America,* Tuttle.